Faith

Angie's Patterns - Volume 6

©2013 Angie Grace. All rights reserved.

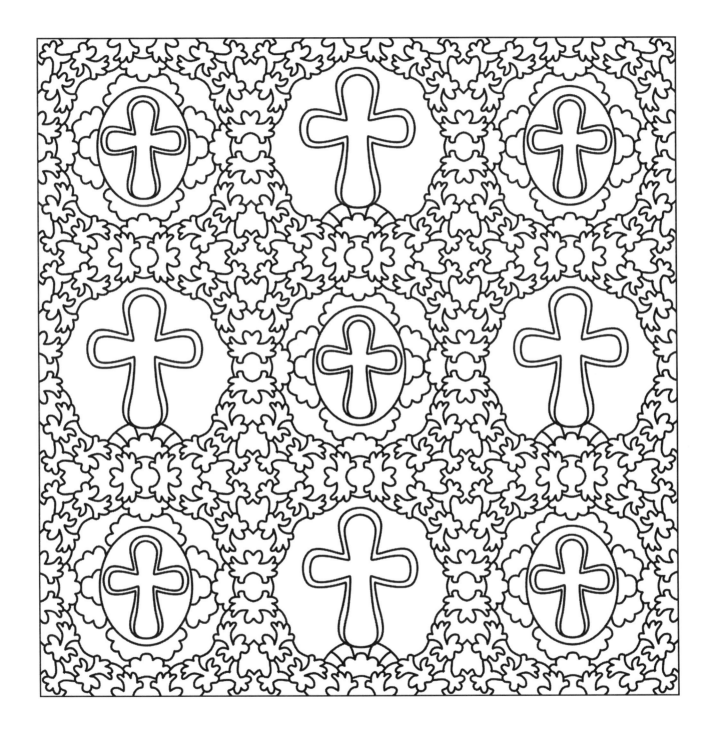

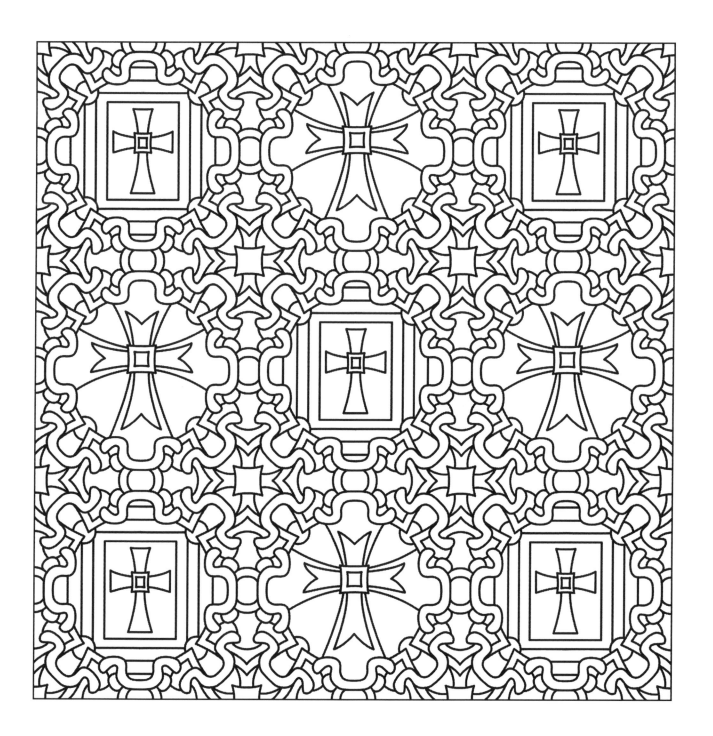

Color With Angie & Friends

Join our friendly Color With Angie Grace Facebook group!

www.AngieGrace.com

Visit Angie's website for special web exclusives for colorists.

Made in the USA
Lexington, KY
23 May 2015